HISTORY CHART

THE WEST FRONT

The great west front of the Cathedral is the first thing most visitors see as they arrive and it is one of the most celebrated of its kind. It resembles an elaborate altar screen and contains an array of carvings which spread across the width of the nave and the towers on either side. This is one of the largest collections of medieval statues in Europe. The lowest niches contain carvings of incidents from the Bible, with scenes from the Old Testament to the right and the New Testament to the left. Above them are knights and ladies, kings and queens, and bishops and saints. At the top are the twelve disciples, with St Andrew, to whom the Cathedral is dedicated, holding his cross in the shape of an X in the middle. Mary, the mother of Jesus, is immediately over the main door, while above everything sits Christ in Majesty (carved in 1985 by David Wynne, to replace a badly worn original).

When the Cathedral was first completed, the west front was painted in bright reds, blues and greens. It was used as a backdrop for religious processions, in particular the one held on Palm Sunday which celebrated the entry of Christ into Jerusalem. On procession days, worshippers crossing the green and entering the Cathedral were greeted with the sounds of trumpets and the voices of choristers coming from specially carved openings between the statues.

Above and right: Details from the West Front

BEGINNINGS

J ust behind the Cathedral, in the grounds of the Bishop's Palace, are the four springs or holy wells which give the city its name. There was probably a shrine here in Roman times, or even earlier, and then a small Christian chapel. In A.D.705 Ine, King of Wessex, gave this land to the Bishop of Sherborne for a church. Sixty years later more royal land was given to 'the Minster beside the great spring called Wiela [Wells] that the priests there may more diligently serve only God in the church of St Andrew the Apostle'. Two hundred years later, in 909, the minster church was raised to the status of cathedral for the county of Somerset. This Saxon building lay to the south of the present one, its east end near the wells and west end opening on to the market place. Its last bishop was Giso (1060-88). His successor John of Tours, who was appointed by William the Conqueror, moved his seat almost immediately to the larger town of Bath, away from the holy, but more remote, town of Wells. Despite its loss of cathedral status, the church continued to have a full complement of clergy and services. The oldest object in the present cathedral is the font, transferred from the Saxon church and now possessing a 17th-century cover. It has been used for Christian baptism for over a thousand years.

Far left: Holy Well *Left:* Saxon font
Above: Part of Saxon tomb cover

THE NEW CATHEDRAL: NAVE

I n about 1175 Bishop Reginald de Bohun ordered work to begin on a new, more splendid church at Wells, on a site just north of the Saxon one. It was to become the first church in England built entirely in the new architectural style known as 'Gothic'.

It would have pointed arches rather than round ones, ceiling vaults which were ribbed rather than barrel-like, and much larger windows. Work began with the quire, on a line between the present pulpit and the bishop's throne, and progressed westwards down the nave, ending with the great west front. Halfway along the nave on the north side is the main entrance, with its high and elaborately decorated porch. Much of the work was done under the master mason Adam Lock, but following his death in 1229 his successor, Thomas Norreys, oversaw the decoration of the West Front.

By 1239 the magnificence of the new church had led Bishop Jocelin to petition the Pope to make Wells once again the seat of the bishop and thus a cathedral. This was authorised in 1245 and the bishop took the title of Bishop of Bath and Wells.

Above: Chantry Chapel
Below: New entry cloister

THE SCISSOR ARCHES

The most striking features of the nave are the long rows of triforium arches just above the pillars on either side of the nave, which draw the eye to the quire screen, and the great 'scissor' arches at the east end. In 1313 a more elaborate storey was added to the top of the central tower, but this had been disastrous and the tower had begun to crack and lean. Between 1338 and 1348 William Joy, the master mason, created the dramatic and successful solution of a scissor arch erected on each of three sides of the crossing under the tower. These, supplemented by hidden buttresses, redistributed the stresses and braced the tower.

The nave was designed as a great space for processions and the only seating was the stone bench around the walls. It was not generally used for services until the 19th century, but is now the setting for special services as well as the principal service each Sunday. The decoration of the ceiling, though restored in 1844 and again in 1985, follows the medieval pattern. In the 15th century two chantry chapels were built at the end of the nave, and the souls of their respective founders were prayed for at special altars.

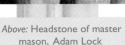
Above: Headstone of master mason, Adam Lock

THE CLOCK

By the end of the 14th century so many services were being held in the Cathedral every day that precise time-keeping became essential. Wells, like other cathedrals, installed a clock, the first record of which dates from 1392. But unlike the other clocks, it is still here. Everything that can be seen of the clock, either inside the building or outside, is medieval. The outer circle is a 24 hour clock, with 12 noon at the top and 12 midnight at the bottom. The second circle marks the minutes in each hour with a small gold star and the third, inner, dial marks the days of the month. A pointer shows the number of days since the New Moon.

As each quarter strikes four horsemen ride round a tower above the clock face, two appearing from each side, as if at a tournament, and one is struck down. The scene is contemporary with the clock but the figures were probably repaired and repainted in the 17th century. So, too, was Jack Blandifer, the figure high on the right. He strikes bells at the hours and quarters with his heels, and marks the hour on the bell in front of him with a hammer.

The statue of the Christus below the clock was carved in yew by Estcourt Clack in 1954.

On the outside wall of the North Transept, near the Chain Gate, are a clock dial and two knights that work off the same mechanism as the inside dial and figures, the knights striking the quarters with their halberds on two bells. The style of their armour dates them to the 15th century. The clock's original medieval mechanism was replaced in 1837 and can now be seen in the Science Museum in London. In 2010 the centuries-old custom of winding the clock by hand came to an end when the task was automated.

Top: The external face of the clock
Above: Jack Blandifer

The building of the Chapter House, which was completed in 1306, was the result of the restoration of Wells to cathedral status. This was the place of business for the Dean and Canons, known collectively as the Chapter. A narrow door from the North Transept leads to a wide curving 'sea of steps' up to the first floor. The additional upper flight, leading over the Chain Bridge to Vicars Hall, was added in the 15th century. The staircase windows hold the oldest stained glass in the Cathedral, dating from c.1290. The Chapter House is octagonal and the vaulted roof has 32 ribs supported by a central pillar, so it resembles a fountain rising from the floor. The huge windows lost most of their original glass when it was smashed in the 17th century, but a few scenes survive in the tracery lights. Round the walls are the Chapter stalls, each with the nameplate of the canon whose vicar (deputy) sat on the lower row of seats at his feet. The carved heads between the arches of the stalls range from king to peasant, from solemn to humorous. Today the full Chapter meets here only on ceremonial occasions, the day-to-day running of the Cathedral being in the hands of the much smaller executive body known as the Administrative Chapter.

Above: Chapter House steps
Right insert: Ceiling boss of 'Green Lady'

Detail of metalwork on a door in the Interpretation Centre

THE INTERPRETATION CENTRE

Below the Chapter House, and a little earlier than it in date, is the Undercroft, a glorious hexagon-shaped space formerly used as the Treasury. It now houses the Interpretation Centre and is open to the public for the first time. Objects and interactive displays tell the story of the Cathedral and enable visitors to explore its architecture, history, art and people, as well as assess its place in the local economy and landscape. The displays offer an insight into everyday life at the Cathedral, including behind-the-scenes glimpses of choir rehearsals, stonemasons at work, vergers preparing the building, organ practice and the bellringing chamber.

The range of objects, from early stone coffins to 17th-century pewter plates, cannon balls to modern mason's tools — still recognisable to his medieval predecessors — aim to stir the imagination and help visitors see the Cathedral through new eyes. The Centre is designed for all ages and is accessible to those with physical and sensory disabilities.

The masons' tools

THE QUIRE

The Quire is, and always has been, at the heart of Cathedral life. Services have been held here daily, almost without a break, since the Cathedral was begun and it is the setting for Choral Evensong today. The Quire was the first part to be built and was probably in use before 1200. Then, between 1320 and 1340, it was extended eastwards to join the existing Lady Chapel. The different architectural style of the three eastern bays beyond the pulpit and bishop's throne marks this extension clearly. The wooden stalls in the Quire were made at the same time. Under each seat is a 'misericord' or wooden carving which supports a small ledge, so that clergy could prop themselves up during long services and rest their weary legs without appearing to sit. The set of 65 surviving carvings is one of the finest in the country. Each was carved from a single piece of oak and consists of a human, animal or fantastical figure subject between two roundels of foliage. The stone canopies of the back stalls were added in 1848, after timber galleries built in the 16th century to provide seating for the families of the clergy were demolished. The richly coloured embroideries were worked in the mid-20th century by a guild of needleworkers.

Above: Misericord showing a sleeping cat
Right: The choir processing

THE JESSE WINDOW
AND THE ORGAN

An important feature of the Quire is the bishop's throne, or 'cathedra', situated opposite the pulpit. It is this which gives the church of St Andrew its status as a cathedral.

The great east window of the Quire dates from about 1340 and is part of the eastward extension. It is known as the Golden Window because of its glowing colours and is among the most splendid 14th-century glass anywhere. It was probably saved from destruction by 17th-century Parliamentary troops by its inaccessibility.

It shows Christ's family tree rising from Jesse, father of King David. Jesse, symbolising Israel, can be seen lying at the bottom of the window with a vine or tree growing from his side. The Madonna and Child are in the centre of the window, immediately above Jesse, flanked by King David with his harp and King Solomon holding a model of the temple he built in Jerusalem.

An organ has stood on the stone 'pulpitum' above the entrance to the Quire since about 1335. The present organ was built by Henry Willis in 1857 and has been rebuilt and enlarged since then, most recently in 1973-4 when the dramatic organ case was built. The gilded wooden angels blowing trumpets date from 1857 as well.

Far left: The bishop's throne
Below left: Jesse Window
Below: Detail of the organ

THE LADY CHAPEL

Every medieval cathedral had its Lady Chapel, built in honour of the mother of Jesus. At Wells the original Lady Chapel adjoined the cloisters. This was destroyed during the Reformation but its remains can still be seen in the Camery Garden. Devotion to the Virgin Mary increased in the 13th and 14th centuries and a new chapel, eight-sided in shape and separate from the main body of the Cathedral, was completed at the east end in 1326. It is important evidence of the medieval fascination with sacred geometry: an elongated octagon when seen from above, from within it appears to be encompassed by a circle. Although separate, the new chapel was precisely aligned with the Quire, and soon after it was completed the Quire was extended eastwards and the Retroquire built to link the two. The upper part of the Lady Chapel windows contain the original glass of *c.*1320-6, but much of the rest is a brilliant jumble of fragments saved when the medieval glass was destroyed during the Civil War (1642-7) and the Monmouth Rebellion (1685).

The roof vault has intricate starburst ribbing of the 1320s but the painted decoration dates from 1845. The modern statue of the Virgin and Child is by A. G. Walker.

Morning Prayer is said here every day.

THE RETROQUIRE, SOUTH QUIRE AISLE AND SOUTH TRANSEPT

The Retroquire was built later in the 14th century to join the Lady Chapel to the Quire, and its graceful forest of pillars links the Quire Aisles, side chapels and Lady Chapel at the east end. The aisles were developed as processional ways and contain more medieval glass, as well as a cope chest dating from the first Saxon cathedral which is still used to store church robes. Also brought from the old cathedral were the bones of seven of the Saxon bishops, whose tombs date from about 1200 and line the North and South Quire Aisles. Fine iron railings of 1450 surround the chantry chapel and tomb of Bishop Thomas Beckynton, who was a great benefactor to the Cathedral and city. His effigy is of painted alabaster and his double-decker tomb, with worldly magnificence above and earthly decay below, is known as a *memento mori* ('Remember you must die').

The South Quire Aisle leads west to the South Transept. This houses the Saxon font and some fine carvings on the 'capitals' at the tops of the pillars. These show scenes from medieval life: someone removing a thorn from his foot, a man with toothache and a cobbler mending shoes. One tells the story of some grape stealers, their capture and punishment, and is like a cartoon strip in stone.

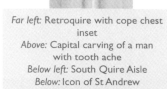

Far left: Retroquire with cope chest inset
Above: Capital carving of a man with tooth ache
Below left: South Quire Aisle
Below: Icon of St Andrew

Wells was never a monastic cathedral, but nonetheless it has a cloister enclosing the Palm Churchyard, the burial place for Cathedral clergy. The 'dipping place' here leads down to the water flowing through a conduit under the cloister, from the wells to the town, which was laid down by Bishop Bekynton in the 15th century. The East Cloister leads to the bishop's entry to his Palace, the doorway once forming part of the narrower 13th-century cloister. Off the cloister are the entrances to the Camery Garden, where the original wells can be viewed, and to the new Education Room, Music School and toilets. Most memorials were moved out of the Cathedral in the 19th century and they now line the cloister walls.

In the 15th century the cloisters were widened to accommodate upper storeys housing the Library and choir schoolroom. The Library over the East Cloister was funded by a bequest from Bishop Nicholas Bubwith (d.1424). It is one of the longest of its period in England and now houses about 6,000 books, some of them still chained to the book presses which date from 1686. The books, which date mainly from the 16th to 18th centuries, reflect the interests of the clergy at that time: not only theology, but law, medicine, exploration, history, travel, languages and science. The Muniment Room at the end of the Library houses the Cathedral's archives from the 11th century.

Below insert: The Hailes Psalter, 1514
Right insert: Entrance from Bishop's Palace

The men who sing in the choir at Wells are called Vicars Choral. They have been a part of Cathedral life since the 12th century. Then, as now, music formed an important part of the services, and busy canons appointed deputies, or 'vicars', to undertake singing duties on their behalf. In 1348 Bishop Ralph of Shrewsbury formed the vicars into a college, built a hall for them to transact their business and eat communally, and provided each of them with a house. Originally there were 42 small houses forming a quadrangle, with a chapel for the vicars at the far end. In the 15th century the Chain Bridge was built to link Vicars' Hall with the Cathedral, and gardens were introduced at much the same time.

After the religious upheavals of the 16th century the number of vicars was reduced and they were allowed to marry, so the houses were put together to form larger dwellings and Vicars' Close took on its present appearance. But throughout the centuries the work of the Vicars Choral continued unchanged. Today, together with the choristers, they sing services every day in term time. They still live in the Close, as do other members of the Cathedral foundation, including the Organist and Master of the Choristers. Some of the houses are used by the Cathedral School, which has a continuous history since its foundation as the medieval choir school.

Far left: Vicars' Hall
Far left below: Chain Gate
Below: Vicars' Close

The successive shrines and churches on this holy site 'next to the great spring' have drawn people into God's presence for over 2,000 years. Today, despite its role as a tourist attraction, the Cathedral remains above all a place of prayer, fulfilling the very same function for which it was built. At least twice a day, on every day of the year, the Cathedral clergy, community and worshippers come together to give thanks to God and pray for the needs of the world. Every day during term time the choir sings Choral Evensong and, as is the case with all services, everyone is welcome. The highly acclaimed choir also sing in concert and CDs of their music are available.

Each year well over 300,000 visitors from home and abroad are welcomed by Cathedral employees and a small army of volunteers. St Benedict said the needs of visitors to a monastery must come before everything else, and in Wells the same principle is followed. The restaurant and shop in the new Entry Cloister cater for their physical needs, while a quiet chapel for prayer and candles for lighting can always be found in the Cathedral itself.

The new Entry Cloister was made possible by the re-opening of a medieval doorway into the West Cloister. It was the culmination of a major development project completed in 2009 which included a new Education Room, Music School and toilets.